THE HIDDEN SECRET

By

CHRISTIAN D. LARSON

Editor of
ETERNAL PROGRESS
AND
THE COSMIC WORLD

1912

L. N. FOWLER & CO.
7, Imperial Arcade, Ludgate Circus, London, E. C.

THE NEW LITERATURE PUBLISHING
COMPANY
Los Angeles, California

Kessinger Publishing's Rare Reprints
Thousands of Scarce and Hard-to-Find Books!

We kindly invite you to view our extensive catalog list at:
http://www.kessinger.net

BY THE SAME AUTHOR

How to Stay Young	$1.00
How to Stay Well	1.00
Business Psychology	1.00
How the Mind Works	1.00
The Ideal Made Real	1.00
What Is Truth	1.00
The Pathway of Roses	1.25
Your Forces and How to Use Them	1.25
Poise and Power	.50
Thinking for Results	.50
Mastery of Fate	.50
The Hidden Secret	.50
The Great Within	.50
Mastery of Self	.50
On the Heights	.50
Just Be Glad	.50
Perfect Health	.50
The Mind Cure	.50
Scientific Training of Children	.50
How Great Men Succeed	.50

The Hidden Secret

To him who has faith all things are possible.

Faith is that something in man that transcends every form of limitation and opens the mind to the limitless powers of the soul.

It is faith that emancipates the person; it is faith that unfolds the unbounded greatness of the soul; it is faith that removes the veil of mystery and reveals to man that wonderful world, that limitless world, that divinely beautiful world that is within.

Faith has been the hidden secret of the great souls in every age; faith has been the secret through which all miracles have been wrought; faith has been the secret through which the prophet gained his wisdom and his power; faith has been the secret through which the sons of glory gained their rare and wonderful genius; faith has been the secret through which everything high, everything worthy and everything beautiful has been given to the world.

It is faith that the awakened minds have eternally sought to find, though not always knowing that the hidden secret was faith, and faith alone; and it is faith that will change the world, as the world should be changed, when its inner sanctuary has been entered by the mind of man.

Faith is the hidden secret to everything; the key that unlocks every door that may exist in the universe; faith is the perfect way to that inner world from which all things proceed; faith is the royal path to unbounded power, immeasurable wisdom and limitless love; faith is the gates ajar to that kingdom which first must be sought if all other things are to be added; faith is the hidden secret to every desire and need of man.

THERE is a faith that *is* faith; there is a faith that can do all things; there is a faith that moves mountains, whatever those mountains may be; there is a faith that rises above every obstacle in the world and reaches the greatest heights that the mind of man may have in view; and it is this faith that is the hidden secret.

When this faith is attained all the ills of human life must take their departure; when this faith is attained every form of poverty must vanish, never to appear again; when this faith is attained every wrong will be righted, the crooked paths made straight, and every wish of the heart satisfied.

This faith is a living faith; it is a faith that works; not a faith that simply consoles. It is not a faith that merely believes things, but a faith that does things.

It is this faith that opens the mind to the limitless possibilities of the great within and gives to man that something through which he may become as great as he ever may desire to be.

It is this faith that the Master Mind referred to when he declared that nothing shall be impossible unto you; it is this faith that gives the word of truth its invincible power; it is this faith that gives birth to the living thought—the thought that has healing on its wings.

It is this faith that will emancipate the race, bring peace on earth, good will to man; and it is this faith that will reveal to mind the hidden spirit of truth—that spirit which, when known, will give man freedom from everything that is human, and the power to attain everything that is divine.

To possess such a faith is the prayer of every spiritual heart, and it is tidings of great joy, indeed, that this prayer may be answered, and answered now.

TO fully define this faith is an effort that will never be attempted, because true faith is far beyond the description of words; the true faith is something that must be spiritually discerned, and the higher one ascends in the understanding of the spirit the larger and more powerful this faith becomes.

Faith is not mere belief; neither is it a doctrine about anything that was, is, or is to be. Faith and belief have nothing in common; they are as different as darkness and light.

Belief is human; faith is more than human; belief knows nothing; faith knows everything.

The true faith is a spiritual state of mind; a state of mind that is very deep, very high, and beautiful beyond description. It is a state of mind that knows; and it knows, because to be in faith is to be upon the mountain-top of intelligence, wisdom and illumination.

The innumerable kingdoms of the great within are known to faith; faith knows everything that is high, everything that is perfect, everything that is limitless, everything that is supreme; faith knows because it has seen; seen with the eyes of the spiritual vision.

Faith is an attitude of mind that turns the superior sense of man towards the inner, the hidden, the unseen, the great beyond, and takes consciousness into those finer realms where everything is perfect, and far more real than that which appears to visible sight.

Faith demonstrates that that which seems unreal is absolutely real; that that which seems hidden can be revealed to any mind, and understood by any mind; and that the invisible becomes visible to all those who will open the full vision that exists within them.

Faith demonstrates that the inner world is far more substantial than the outer world, and that the farther we proceed into the great within the more substantial, the more real, the more perfect and the more beautiful everything becomes.

One of the principal functions of faith is to enter the boundless and awaken the great within; and since all increase in life, power and ability comes from the awakening of a larger and a larger measure of the within, we understand perfectly why all things are possible to him who has faith.

THERE is a life within that has no limit; it is the life more abundant—the life that every awakened mind has sought with heart and soul; it is the life from which all great things proceed; the source of everything that has real value and high worth.

Faith opens the door to this life and takes man into the sacred sanctuary within. To enter this life is to be filled with this life, and gain possession of all that this life may contain.

This does not indicate that faith deals wholly with a life that is apart from daily life; faith finds real life—abundance of real life, and what it finds it gives richly to daily life. Faith opens the mind to the influx of limitless life, and every atom in one's being becomes filled with this life.

Faith does not dwell apart from things, but works through things, giving to all things an abundance of the unbounded power from within. Without the spirit of faith, things become lifeless, soulless, purposeless, useless.

Everything is limited when faith is absent; everything breaks bounds when faith appears.

Faith does not work apart from intellect, but gives soul to intellect; illumines the intellect with higher wisdom; inspires the intellect with greater possibilities; permeates the intellect with a power that mind can never measure.

Faith not only gives superiority to the intellect, but elevates the mind to a higher and higher state of comprehension, so that an ever-increasing world of thought and life is incorporated in the scope of mentality. This gives added power and quality to every talent, and opens consciousness to the limitless source of everything that mind may require.

HATEVER we may desire to accomplish, nothing is more important than to possess that rare faculty called resourcefulness. To be able to draw upon the limitless for thought, ideas, plans, methods, wisdom, power, inspiration, in brief, everything that one may require to take advantage of every opportunity—to be able to do this is to be able to reach the highest goal that mind may have in view.

And faith enables the mind to do this; faith opens all the doors to everything that mind may desire to secure; faith opens the mind to that immense inner world from which everything may be received.

It is being demonstrated more fully every day that all things pertaining to the life of man come from the within; not only great things, but all things. From the within comes all wisdom, and the mind that has awakened the largest measure of the within has the greatest wisdom.

The same is true of power; we do not receive power from what we eat or drink, nor from the air we breathe; power comes from an inner world; therefore, he who would become strong in body, mind and soul must awaken more and more of the great within.

That rare insight—that something that leads and guides with a superhuman understanding—that also comes from the illumined within, and develops as consciousness gains a higher realization of the inner world. By entering this superior state of mind one will live perpetually in the light, and thereby eliminate all mistakes from daily existence. And he who enters faith enters this superior, illumined state.

The other forms of understanding, perception, conception, and comprehension also have their source in the inner mind, and will increase in power and efficiency as the within unfolds.

The powers that create, the forces that build, the elements that promote the growth of mind and soul—all of these come from the same inner source, and will come in greater abundance as the inner world is awakened in the mind of man.

The love that loves everything with real love also comes from the wonderful within; likewise, purity, virtue, kindness, harmony, joy and the peace that passeth understanding. All of these may be obtained in boundless supply through the living of life in faith.

Every form of health and wholeness,

and all perfect conditions of mind or body have their origin in the within; therefore, he who would banish all the ills of life must, through faith, unfold the perfect life from that limitless, inner world.

Whatever we may require for attainment, advancement, or the enlargement of life, we may secure from the great within; and since faith is the royal path to this marvelous realm, we understand again why all things are possible to him who has faith.

O obtain complete emancipation, to perpetually ascend in the scale of life, to become something, to accomplish something, to secure results, to do things, to move forward, to make every effort count, to make the fullest use of everything that one may be, or possess, to live a life worth while and to secure from life the very best that life has the power to give—these are some of the ruling desires among the better minds of to-day; and we know of no desires that are more worthy, nor more indicative of a superior understanding of real existence.

It is therefore a great privilege to gain possession of that something through which all of these desires may be realized; and since that something is faith, everyone may henceforth fulfill his desires—all of his desires, because anyone can obtain faith. In fact, everyone has faith, to a degree; when anyone ceases to have faith he will cease to be. Before man can do anything he must have faith; he must have faith even before he can begin to perpetuate existence.

To live is to move forward; to do anything, or attempt anything is to move forward; and to move forward is to enter the great unknown—unknown to the senses, but not to faith. Faith knows that the seeming void of the great unknown is solid rock; faith knows that man may safely proceed, and by what faith man may possess he does proceed.

If there was nothing within him to give him this assurance, this *feeling* that he may proceed with safety, he would not proceed; he would bring the whole of existence to a stand-still, and cease to be.

This, however, no one will ever do, because faith is a part of the soul; it is inseparably united with the soul; one can never lose all his faith, but one can increase its power without end; and as the power of faith is increased, by having more faith, the expression of life will increase, and everything that comes from life will increase.

The life of man is large or small in proportion to his faith, because it is through faith that he touches the source of life and receives life.

Likewise, all the attainments and achievements of man are large or small in proportion to his faith. "According to your faith," that is the law that determines everything.

Since faith is the hidden secret of all life, and is absolutely indispensable to existence, we all have faith just as we all have life; to find faith, we are therefore not required to search for something we never knew; we are simply required to have more faith in the faith we already possess; the greater things will invariably follow.

THROUGH faith every desire can be realized, and every object in view can be accomplished, because faith places mind in touch with the power that can do all things.

Faith opens the mind to the unbounded power from within and creates in mind the conscious realization of that power. When you are *in* faith the power that you feel is so great that nothing seems impossible; you feel strong enough to do almost anything, and what you feel is the truth.

You *can* do anything while you are absolutely in faith, because while you are in faith you are in a world where unlimited power is at your command.

There is a world of limitless power; that world is within us and all about us, but in ordinary consciousness we are not aware of its existence; at those times, however, when we transcend ordinary consciousness we gain glimpses of this marvelous world.

It is during such moments that we feel strong enough to move mountains; it is then that we receive our inspirations, when new truths are revealed, when new discoveries are made, and when immortal deeds are done.

This world of limitless power is an inner world permeating the outer world, and is revealed through faith; it is through faith that we enter into this world, and it is through the growth of faith that we realize its limitless power, thereby gaining possession of a greater measure of this power.

The fact that we live and move and have our being in a world of unlimited power, that we can become conscious of this world through faith, and thereby place unlimited power at our command—the fact that this is the truth is a fact so extraordinary, so far-reaching and so enormously important that it should be proclaimed with a loud voice to all the world; and not a single soul should live another day without hearing this wonderful message proclaimed.

This is one of the greatest truths of all truths, and should not only receive profound attention from every mind, but it is a truth that should be constantly held in every mind. To live, think and act in the spirit of this truth—*the truth that you live and move and have your being in a world of unlimited power and that through faith all of this power is placed at your command*—to live in this truth, with faith, is to open the mind more and more to the perpetual influx of this power, until you gain so much of this power that nothing becomes impossible to you henceforth and forever.

That there is such a world no one can doubt; that faith is the hidden path to that world anyone can demonstrate; anyone can also demonstrate that we gain possession of an immense power while we are in that world, and that the power continues to be our own so long as we remain *in* the full faith; it is therefore evident that those who will continue permanently *in* the full faith will accomplish everything they may undertake to do.

Through the growth of faith—the real faith, the mind becomes more and more aware of this inner world, and consciousness opens more and more to receive its limitless power; the entire personality becomes filled with the power, and ere long you *feel* that an immense power is with you every moment of existence. This brings the realization that nothing is impossible; you never hesitate to undertake anything that is worthy, no matter how great and extensive the undertaking may be, because you *know* there is a power with you that can do all things. You feel that this power is working through you; you feel that it is your power; therefore, anything worthy that you may undertake, the same shall be done.

To enter this realization is to gain more

power from the very beginning; therefore, he who enters faith will begin at once to accomplish greater things and better things, whatever his work may be; and as for his future, it is as great, as wonderful and as beautiful as he may desire to make it.

BY entering the immensity of superior mental worlds, faith enlarges the mind, thereby increasing capacity, ability and every substantial quality contained in the world of intelligence.

Through the same process faith expands consciousness beyond all present limitations and adds rich domains to the kingdom of mentality. To live in faith is to live a larger and a greater life perpetually, because it is the nature of faith to enlarge, expand and develop everything that pertains to the mental and spiritual life of man.

Faith penetrates the great unknown and makes it known; faith goes out upon the seeming void and finds the solid rock; faith always finds the solid rock because the solid rock is everywhere.

Everything is real and substantial; the fathomless depths and the immeasurable heights contain worlds within worlds; all real, all substantial, all perfectly safe for mind to enter and explore. Faith knows this, therefore never hesitates to go out upon the seeming void; never hesitates to go on with every worthy undertaking.

Faith knows that all is real and all is possible, and acts accordingly.

Faith demonstrates conclusively that you may go out in every direction, or enter into any depth of soul-existence, you will find the Infinite everywhere; you will find real life everywhere; you will find beautiful souls everywhere; you will find love and peace everywhere; and wherever you go you will find unlimited possibilities, unbounded power, and innumerable opportunities to arise in the endless scale of existence.

Again it is most evident that all things are possible to him who has faith.

Through the action of faith new worlds are discovered in every part of mentality, and valuable qualities, talents, capabilities and powers constantly added. Through the revelations of faith we discover that the most prodigious minds we know are but infants compared with what we all may become now, if we will simply have faith in faith, and follow faith into these greater mental worlds that we even touch at every movement of thought.

We are all on the very verge of rare genius, superior talent and limitless worlds of extraordinary intelligence; but faith alone can lead us on; faith alone is the hidden secret to the wisdom and power that knows no bounds.

Every faculty of the mind can be enlarged and expanded indefinitely; there is no end to the possibilities that may be unfolded and developed through the enlargement of the various faculties of the outer mind; even the physical senses may expand their spheres of action far beyond the widest stretches of the imagination.

The world of color, the world of sound, the world of feeling—all the worlds of sense are limitless. That the physical senses have limitations is not the truth; they may appear to be limited because they have not been developed beyond their present spheres of action; but through faith we discover that the spheres of action of the physical senses contain possibilities for enlargement that have absolutely neither limitation nor end.

Through faith we also discover how this development of the senses may be promoted on the largest possible scale.

Innumerable kingdoms of marvelous beauty lie hidden within the world of color; the same is true of the world of sound; and as to the possibilities that are latent in the sense of feeling, we have not dreamed of a millionth part.

We may think the world is beautiful; and it is, but our perception of the beautiful is in its first stages only; it remains for the further development of physical sight and the discernment of color to reveal to us worlds of splendor such as mind has never been able to picture.

We may be charmed into ecstasy with certain tender strains of music, but the sweetest music is not heard; the most tender strains do not touch the soul; we pass them by, not even knowing of their existence. The world of sound with its innumerable symphonies is almost entirely closed to the average mind. He may be charmed with what little he does hear, but what will he be when he hears it all?

It is through the further development of the physical senses that many of these beautiful worlds will be realized and enjoyed; and it is through faith that the physical senses will reach that higher state of development; because it is faith that enters the unknown; it is faith that penetrates the within; it is faith that transcends all limitations and gives to mind greater and greater measures of the immensities still in store.

Faith is the secret to all that is hidden; and to him who follows faith, all things will be revealed.

What faith can do for the enlargement of the physical senses and the outer mind, it can do far more extensively for the spiritual senses and the inner mind. We therefore understand perfectly why all things are possible to him who has faith.

WE all realize that unlimited possibilities are latent in the great within; and we are all in search of the best and most thorough methods through which these possibilities may be developed; but it has been discovered that the within is unfolded only through the expansion of consciousness; how to expand consciousness, therefore, becomes one of the greatest problems in the life of man.

It is solved, however, through faith; faith expands consciousness; in fact, it is only through faith that consciousness may be expanded. This is a fact of extreme importance, a fact that every metaphysician and psychologist should note with care, and act accordingly. The absence of real faith among psychologists is the reason why the greatest part of their efforts are of no practical value to the world; and the deficiency in faith among metaphysicians is the reason why all the sick are not healed, why all who have troubles do not secure complete emancipation.

Add faith, real faith, to practical metaphysics, and failures among those who are seeking to remove the ills of human life, would almost entirely disappear.

Do not simply speak the word of truth, but have faith in the truth and the truth shall make you free.

It is not the literal statement of truth, but the soul of truth that contains the healing power, the emancipating power, the power that can do all things; and when we have faith we enter the soul of truth.

That we must have faith before we can become conscious of the new, the larger, the better, the higher, the spirit of things, is very evident when we realize that it is faith alone that goes out upon the seeming void; it is faith alone that breaks bounds and demonstrates the existence of a greater life; it is faith that takes the first step forward always, but wherever faith may go, consciousness invariably follows.

We therefore understand clearly that to awaken the great within, and develop the unlimited possibilities that are latent within us, faith is the hidden secret.

Through faith the mind gains a greater comprehension of all things, whether those things be physical, intellectual or spiritual.

The greater the faith the larger the view and the better the view, whatever the subject of thought may be; and the more thorough the understanding. Faith is therefore a priceless gift to every mind in existence; for there is no place in life where faith will not be a great and wonderful power for good.

Through faith the mind ascends into that state of being where the life more abundant—the spiritual life, the eternal life—is realized and received; and among all the powers of faith, this is the greatest.

The unfoldment of the inner life prepares the way for the unfoldment of the soul, and places every high spiritual attainment within reach of the growing mind.

Among the many methods that have been given for soul-unfoldment, pure spiritual faith is by far the greatest; other methods may become aids to faith, but without faith they have no value.

A great truth to remember is this, that no soul-unfoldment or spiritual development is possible without faith; and that no system of higher culture or attainment has any value whatever unless it is based upon faith.

FAITH awakens the new life, the healing life, the emancipating life, the purifying life, the regenerating life, the life that *is* power, health, wholeness and freedom; therefore, through faith anyone may attain complete emancipation from all the ills of human existence.

The coming of the strong, pure life from within will dispel every form of physical disease or mental distress, as light dispels the darkness; and to have faith is to open the entire human personality to the coming of those higher powers of the soul that have healing on their wings.

No disease can remain in the system after these higher spiritual forces have come forth into mind and body; and whenever the real, interior faith is entered into, these forces are awakened with all their purity and power.

When disease threatens, have faith; and have faith in faith; feel the very soul of faith in every atom of your being and the healing power of the soul will fill your system through and through.

Faith is the hidden secret to the power that can do all things; therefore, to have faith in faith is to enter the hidden life of that power; to feel the very spirit of that life, and to permeate that spirit with every conscious action of mind.

When we realize that faith is the hidden secret, and enter into the innermost life of that secret with every thought we think, the invincible powers within will awaken at once; and whatever we desire to do, the same will be done.

The effect of faith upon the intellect is most beneficial in every way; the reason being that the attitude of faith elevates mind above all confusion, doubt, fear, uncertainty and limitations, and actually illumines the entire mental domain.

To enter faith is to enter the crystal sea of pure intelligence, and to steadily grow into that superior understanding that knows because it *is* the light of truth and wisdom.

He who lives constantly in the attitude of faith will, ere long, develop remarkable intellectual brilliancy.

He who lives in faith will not only increase his ability, and the power that does things, but will also acquire that rare and most excellent faculty of doing the right thing at the right time. Faith does develop higher mental insight, thus giving mind the power to act with real wisdom, keen judgment and superior understanding.

AITH is the hidden secret to the real, the true, the genuine and the superior in all things; therefore, to enter faith is to gain possession of the highest truth about everything.

Faith ignores all the limitations of objective intelligence and enters the larger mental world of superior intelligence; faith knows that the dark unknown will be found to be filled with light after we have entered its luminous splendor, and by entering this more brilliant mental world, faith proves that its faith was true.

In the development of the various mental faculties faith is indispensable; the reason for such a far-reaching statement is found in the fact that it is the finer creative energies of mind that build talents; and that we must enter the inner mental world to awaken those energies; but it is only through faith that consciousness can reach the inner realms of mind.

When we are in faith we are in the conscious realization of the finer forces— those forces that are required in every form of physical, mental or spiritual development.

Faith is the hidden secret to all the

higher powers; therefore, when we enter faith we enter the conscious possession of those powers, and may employ them for any purpose that is before us now.

As we grow in faith the finer creative energies increase in power, because the more faith we have the more power we receive from within; we thereby promote the development of talent, genius and rare ability on an ever-increasing scale.

In the development of any faculty the circumscribed must be transcended, and that phase of consciousness that acts within the faculty must be widened and heightened; this faith does invariably, thereby, not only giving every faculty a larger sphere of action, but also greater power and superior quality.

The higher consciousness ascends in the mental world of any faculty, the higher and finer becomes the quality of that faculty; and since faith always promotes the ascension of consciousness, superior mental quality will invariably follow the attainment of faith.

This truth will be better understood when we realize that the larger, the greater and the superior is to be found in the within on a higher plane, and that to gain possession of the superior we must develop the consciousness of the within; that is, consciousness must be expanded to such an extent that it reaches into the within and comprehends the within as well as the without.

Since faith is the only path to the within, and since it is only through faith that consciousness can be expanded, faith therefore becomes indispensable to all forms of development.

Faith is the hidden secret to the true, the perfect and the limitless in everything; therefore, to find faith is to find everything. Nothing is hidden from him who has faith, because he who enters into faith enters into that which was hidden, and it is hidden no more.

Since faith is a hidden path, it can be entered into only when our thinking enters the inner meaning of faith, and as a conscious effort is made to inwardly feel faith.

By concentrating attention upon the inner meaning of faith, trying to feel the spirit of faith, we find the path to faith and steadily enter more deeply into the real soul of faith.

To exercise faith is to consciously enter the inner and the finer essence of everything in which we may have faith; not to mentally dwell on the surface of things, but to dwell on the inner life of things— the hidden secret of things.

When we understand the inner meaning

of faith, and realize that faith is the hidden secret, the mere thought of faith will take the mind into faith; while in faith the mind is opened to the unbounded powers that come through faith, and all limitations and seeming impossibilities disappear from consciousness completely.

When we exercise faith, all doubt, all fear and all anxiety are absent; should these undesirable mental states appear, we may know that our minds are thinking about the surface of things instead of the spirit of things.

To be in faith is to think about the spirit of things, to mentally dwell within the spirit of things, to *feel* the spirit of things and to be filled through and through with the unbounded power of this spirit.

Faith never pays any attention to appearances; faith has information from a higher source; faith knows that all things are possible now, because to be in faith is to be *in* that power that can do all things now.

When we try to enter faith we must give full right-of-way to this power; we must permit this power to thrill every atom in being, and we must give this power the privilege to do whatever we now may desire to have done.

The more we depend upon this power the

more of this power we shall receive, until our capacity becomes enormous.

The more we exercise faith the more faith we shall secure; and the more faith we have in faith the more deeply we shall enter into the very soul of faith.

TO secure the largest and best possible results from the practical application of faith, it is necessary to have a perfect faith in everything with which we may come in contact, both on the visible and invisible sides of life.

Have faith in yourself, have faith in man, have faith in the universe, have faith in God, and have faith in faith.

To have faith in everything is to develop the power of faith in every direction, and it is the full faith that opens the mind to the power that can do all things.

The principal reason why faith sometimes fails is because we exercise faith in some things while we have doubts about others.

It is the faith that has faith in all things and at all times that is real faith; and it is the faith that has faith in the full faith that makes all things possible.

There is a power for good in everything; in everything something may be found that has true value and real worth; something that can add to the welfare of man; but this something is found, not on the surface, but within the soul of things. It is therefore necessary to enter into perfect touch with the inner life of everything to secure the best from everything; and this is possible only through faith.

When we have faith in all things we enter into absolute oneness with the real life of all things; we place ourselves in touch with the universal, and may consequently draw upon the limitless for anything the heart may desire.

The universal can supply all things; therefore, he who lives constantly in perfect touch with the universal will never want for anything.

When you have faith in yourself you awaken the immensity of your own interior life, and bring into expression your better self, your superior self, your limitless self.

There is something in man that is more than human; something that is far greater than the personal man; something that transcends every form of visible existence; something that is created in the image of the Supreme; and it is faith that unfolds this higher being, causing the Word to become flesh, thereby permeating the visible form with the beauty and the divinity of the soul.

It is the nature of faith to enter the higher, the larger and the boundless; therefore, by living in faith you will mentally dwell in a growing consciousness of superiority. This will develop superiority in all your talents and faculties, because whatever we become conscious of, that we express through our own mind and character.

Have faith in yourself and you will always be at your best; you will constantly express the best that exists in your conscious nature, and your work will be the result of your greatest capacity and highest efficiency.

By having full and constant faith in yourself you place every part of your system in the best possible working condition; and besides, you promote in yourself the process of continuous improvement.

To live in faith is to move forward every single moment; because it is one of the functions of faith to press on—to ceaselessly press on.

The man who has the most faith in himself invariably does the best work, and consequently secures the most remunerative places in the industrial world. Faith elevates mind to the highest state of ability and awakens the necessary power from within to sustain the high position.

The man who continues to have a perfect faith in himself can never fail, because it is worth that wins, and faith never ceases to develop worth.

By having faith in yourself you bring

to the surface the best that you possess, and then proceed to gain conscious possession of better talents and greater powers than you have ever known before.

There is a genius asleep in the subconscious of every mind; in the great within of every mind, unbounded capacity and ability may be found; and it is faith that awakens this genius; it is faith that unfolds the limitless possibilities within.

Faith is the hidden secret to greatness, because faith takes man into the inner life of that power that produces greatness. Therefore, he who has faith in himself may become anything, attain anything and accomplish anything.

To have faith in yourself is to *feel* the life and power of that something within yourself that is limitless; that something that is created in the image and likeness of the Supreme.

To grow in that faith, never think of the surface of your system, but think of the strong soul that permeates every atom of your being; mentally dwell upon the inner side of your life, and train your thought to act only upon the finer energies, the finer substance and the real spirit that fills your body, mind and soul.

To develop faith in yourself have faith in the faith that declares that you are the image and likeness of the Supreme, therefore limitless. Aim to be your best and live in the faith that you always will be your best; then have faith in your every word, your every thought and your every deed.

Most important of all, whenever you try to have faith, whenever you think of faith, *mentally feel* the inner meaning of faith. This will invariably produce results.

HEN we have faith in man we enter into the most harmonious relations with the better side of man; we mentally live with the real man, the superior man, the true man. We consequently will think, not of human weakness, but of the supreme power and the divine life that exists in man.

What we constantly recognize in others we develop in ourselves; and we steadily grow into the likeness of that which we think of the most.

When we have faith in all people we attract better people, and will have the privilege to live with those who are as we wish them to be.

What we constantly hold in mind that we invariably attract to ourselves; and when we have faith in man it is the better man, the real man, the true man that receives our undivided attention. We shall consequently have the privilege to associate with those who express the real and the true in the highest and most perfect measure.

He who has the most faith in mankind has the most friends and the best friends; he receives the truest love from the largest number, and the best that the world can give will constantly flow into his life.

When we have faith in others we inspire others to have faith in themselves; they, consequently, become more competent and more highly developed, thereby helping to make life better for everybody concerned.

The more faith we have in people the more they will do for us, the more they will do for themselves, and the more valuable they become to the whole world.

Have faith in the world, and the wrongs of the world will be righted. Have faith in everybody, and you inspire everybody to have faith in everybody; and when everybody has faith in everybody, sin, sorrow and sickness will vanish from this planet.

This is a scientific statement, because when we all have faith in each other, the life of the whole race will be a living faith; the life of every person will be lived in faith, and to live in faith is to live in that life that knows neither sickness, sorrow nor sin. To live in faith is to enter the life of that pure spiritual power that not only can, but does, banish the ills of human existence.

When things seem to go wrong, do not complain about the incompetence of man, but have faith in man, and the better side of everybody with which you are connected, will appear to set all matters right.

The complaining mind goes down into more confusion and denser mental darkness, thereby making more mistakes and misleading everybody concerned to a lesser or greater extent.

It is the truth that the more we complain the more we shall find about which to complain; and the more we contend with things the more things we shall have with which to contend.

The more faith we have in man when in the midst of adversity, the sooner we shall find the way out, and the sooner we shall find the help required under the circumstances.

Faith keeps the eye single upon the better, the right and the true; and he who keeps the eye single upon the better rises into the realization of the better. This is an absolute law through the use of which any one may find emancipation; and faith is the hidden secret to that law and its perfect use.

The man who has faith in everybody will never have much to complain about; the best of everything will come with him into his way, and all things will work together for his good.

There is nothing that will smoothen the pathway of life, and harmonize all the conditions of life more perfectly and more rapidly than a full, strong, living faith—a faith that has faith in everybody and in everything.

When we have faith in everything we are brought into closer touch with the best of everything, and will thus secure the best from every source.

This is perfectly natural, because whenever we enter into the life of faith we enter into the best, the highest and the truest that there is in life. Faith lives in the superior world, and to enter into faith is to enter that world.

What we enter into with mind, that we become conscious of; and what we become conscious of, that we express through our own mentalities and personalities. Therefore, by entering the inner realms of superiority we develop in ourselves all the qualities of superiority.

HAVE faith in your work, and your efforts will produce far greater results; because through the attitude of faith you give your very best life and power to your work. In addition you enter into a more perfect harmony with all the elements contained in your work, thereby producing that unity of purpose which invariably culminates in great achievements.

Have faith in every opportunity and the richest treasures that may be hidden within that opportunity will be given to you. Faith enters the soul of things and gains possession of the very essence of all worth. Wherever there is a secret, faith will find it.

Have faith in every circumstance, in every phase of environment and these will give only their best to you. When you have faith, averse environments will trouble you no more; they will, on the other hand, become open gates to pastures green.

Nothing but the best can come through faith, therefore it is the hidden secret to the best that anything in the world can give.

If you cannot understand this, have

faith, and faith will reveal to you the reason why. The hidden secret of faith is revealed only to those who live *in* faith.

Have faith, even in adversity; believe with the whole heart that adverse circumstances are simply opportunities to a larger life for you; and as your faith is so shall it be.

There is a power in every form of adversity—a power that can be turned to good account. Faith enters into harmony with this power, gains possession of it and transforms adversity into a most powerful friend.

Live in the faith that all things are working out right, and you will draw all things into the pathway of right; all things will go with you and do the right things for you.

There is nothing strange about this, because the power of faith is invincible. Faith is in touch with the world of unbounded power, therefore can do all things.

Have faith in all the elements and forces of nature, and their hidden secrets shall be revealed to you. Faith can find anything; faith goes into the soul of things, and through superior vision discerns everything that may exist in life.

Live perpetually in the full faith, and you shall discover many things that the world has never known; things that may add immeasurably to the welfare of the race.

When we have faith in all things our attention is subconsciously concentrated upon the best; we thereby think the best, create the best, and enter into the world of the best. By entering into the world of the best we shall have the privilege to associate with the best, appropriate the best and live the best.

The secret of high thinking and right thinking is therefore found in faith; and as man is as he thinks we again realize the unbounded value of faith.

WHEN we have faith in God we enter into oneness with God, and with everything in the universe that is good.

It is only through faith that we may know God; it is only through faith that we may enter the presence of God and walk with God; it is only through faith that we may enter the spirit and dwell in the secret places of the Most High.

Faith removes the gulf that seems to exist between God and man by demonstrating that there is no gulf, but that man is One with God now, in the highest, truest and fullest sense of divine unity.

To enter faith is to know that "My Father and I are one", and to feel that the power to do the greater things are even now at hand.

To enter faith is to enter into the conscious realization of the great truth that man is created in the image and likeness of God; to enter faith is to inwardly feel that "I am the Son of God," and that "all that the Father hath is mine."

When we have faith in God we are *with* God, and realize perfectly that to him who is *with* God all things are possible.

No one can fail when God is with him;

and God is with everybody who unites his mind with the Infinite mind.

"Come with Me, and I am with thee," thus speaketh the Voice Divine in the soul of every man.

Those who have faith can hear this voice, and will invariably act accordingly.

Have faith in God and you will live with God, and you will *feel* that God is with you in everything you may undertake to do.

Do not simply believe in God. *Have faith in God.* The difference is immense.

He who simply believes in God stands apart from God; but he who has faith in God enters into the very spirit of God; he is filled with the power of God; the purity of God; the wisdom of God and the peace of God; and he rests eternally in the arms of Infinite Love.

To have faith in God is to take God absolutely at His Word; to believe so thoroughly that all things are created in the image of God, and that all things are good, because created by God, that we proceed to act accordingly.

Everything that God has created is good, and he who lives in faith finds that all things are good.

He also finds that the imperfections of man's creations disappear completely when we realize the perfections of God's creations.

When we have faith in God we can doubt nothing; we know that infinite power, infinite wisdom and infinite love are within all things, and that the final results will be wonderful, marvelous, indescribably beautiful.

When we have faith in God our fears and worries disappear; what we ourselves can not overcome or accomplish, we place in the hands of God, living in the faith that God *can* and *will* make all things well; and as our faith is, so it is always done unto us.

When you feel that you live and move and have your being in God you will never have any fear; you know that you are safe and secure; fully protected at all times; and that nothing but good can come to you. Again, as your faith is, so is it done unto you.

To eliminate fear of every sort, simply have faith in God; it is a remedy that never fails. Glad tidings of great joy, indeed; something that is worth all the wisdom in the world.

Again, do not simply believe in God; *have faith in God.*

When you have faith in God you enter so completely into the spirit of God that you actually *feel* that He is "closer than breathing, nearer than hands and feet."

To be in this state is not only supreme

joy, but it is to be in a state of superior wisdom, superior ability and superior power.

While in this state you realize that "My Father worketh and I work." You feel that the hand of the Infinite works with your hand, and that neither weariness nor failure can possibly follow.

While in this state, you think the thoughts of the Infinite after Him; your mind is illumined with the Word of wisdom, and the spirit of Truth reigns supremely in all your world. You are in the peace that passeth understanding; you have forgotten evil because you know only the good; you are within the pearly gates and are living with the souls of shining glory.

You have entered that state wherein the Christ entered when his face did shine as the sun, and his garments were white as the light.

You have entered the presence of God, you have been glorified with His spirit and His love; you have seen His Kingdom—God's perfect world—that world in which we all may dwell *now,* providing we not simply believe in God, but *have faith in God.*

TO find the hidden secret of faith the principal secret is to have faith in faith.

To have faith in faith is to enter into the very soul of faith, thereby increasing all the powers of faith, and giving mind that inner secret through which everything that is great and extraordinary may be accomplished.

To develop the power of faith, realize that faith is the hidden secret; then direct the whole of attention upon the soul of the hidden secret until you feel that you are in the very life of life itself.

While you are in the very *life* of life, you are *in* faith; it is then that you have faith in faith because you are within the within; you are in the secret chamber of the hidden secret; you are in the spirit of the very soul of all existence.

It is in this state that you find the perfect peace, the limitless power and the supreme joy. It is in this state that you find the beautiful calm, the heaven within and the life eternal. It is in this state that the personal will gives way to the divine will, and where we can hear the gentle voice, "Ask what thou wilt and I will answer thee."

To be in this state is to have faith in faith; we can therefore understand why all things are possible to him who has faith; and why all things shall be according to our faith.

HATEVER you attempt while you have faith in faith that you shall surely accomplish; the power of faith is limitless, and to have faith in faith is to work *in* the limitless power of faith.

To gain that understanding of truth that knows the real truth—the truth that makes man free, the secret is to have faith in faith. More real wisdom comes through having faith in faith than through all other sources combined; though the other sources must not be neglected.

The usual sources of knowledge supply the body, the vehicle, the instrument of wisdom; faith supplies the light, the power, the life, the soul of wisdom.

By having faith in faith our own faith becomes stronger, larger, higher and more perfect, until we are *in* real faith; and to be in real faith is to be within the gates of the soul's unbounded domain; to be within the very innermost chamber of life; to be in the spirit itself.

It is therefore evident that nothing can be impossible to him who has faith; and the perfect path to more faith is to have faith in everything and to have faith in that faith.

To have faith in faith is to keep the eye single upon the greater in every kingdom of life; to open the mind to see the greater in all things. The mind that is constantly seeing the greater is constantly entering into the greater, and is therefore eternally becoming greater.

The thoughts we create while in faith are always strong, because the attitude of faith gives higher power to everything; more evidence to prove that faith can do all things.

Faith enlarges all the faculties and spheres of action in the mind of man, and expands consciousness to such an extent that it perpetually breaks bounds and penetrates even those realms that objective man has never known.

The mind that has faith may discover anything at any time, because faith dwells eternally upon the borderland of greater things. Therefore, to develop the power of faith train consciousness to act constantly upon the borderland of the unknown; and train every action of mind to touch the limitless in every part of mental life.

In all these actions, however, the mind must act in faith and must inwardly feel that the seeming void everywhere is solid rock. This removes all timidity about pressing on, into the great unknown, and makes the great unknown a splendid world of reality, even more real than the world that is tangible to the physical senses.

Faith has no fear because faith does not grope blindly in the dark; faith knows; faith can see; faith is in the light and demonstrates that the entire universe is full of light. Through faith we can see much farther than we can reach, therefore know how to proceed. We know where to go, how to go and when to go in order to enter the greater life, the more beautiful life—the life that is fairer than ten thousand to the soul.

Every step in advance that may be taken is the result of faith; it is faith only that can lead mind on into larger realms, superior ability and greater powers; therefore, we should give faith the full credit for every increase that appears in life. By doing this the power of faith will increase; and as we receive more faith we shall receive more of everything else that is good in the world.

When faith grows, all good things grow, and there is nothing that promotes the growth of faith more rapidly than to give faith credit for what faith has done; and without faith nothing has been done.

Nothing is accomplished without faith, because every step taken in advance must be preceded by the faith that it is possible.

Faith always leads the way; nor does

faith disappear with the improvement of the intellect; it is faith that makes it possible for the intellect to improve. What faith sees the intellect enters into and proceeds to analyze, understand and comprehend; but the intellect never goes where faith has not first revealed a new world of possibility to study and explore.

THE greatest power that can be expressed through the mind of man comes from the united actions of desire and faith. This power is actually irresistible; therefore, whatever we desire in faith, that we shall positively receive.

Have faith, and no true desire shall remain unfulfilled; not that we shall always receive the very identical thing desired, because that would frequently prove undesirable; but the desire will be fulfilled. When we do not receive the very thing desired we shall receive something that will serve our purpose far better.

When we express a strong desire, and leave it to faith to fulfill that desire, the very best will be secured; faith lives in a higher light and can see far better than the personal man what would give us the greatest good and the greatest joy. Faith, therefore, acts accordingly, when we have faith in faith, and does not always give us what we ask for, but gives us something better.

The prayer of faith is always answered, and it is the only prayer that is always answered.

The true prayer is the prayer that is expressed while we are in the spirit; and since it is the function of faith to open the way to the spirit and take us into the spirit, the prayer of faith will always be in the spirit.

To pray is not to stand apart and ask God, but to take our desires to God; to enter into the presence of God and receive directly through the spirit whatever we may desire and need.

The prayers that are sent to a distant God are never answered; but the prayers that we personally take to God, through faith, these prayers are always answered. To ask for something is not the only essential in prayer; we must personally enter into the presence of God and personally receive the answer.

To receive from the Infinite what we may desire, or pray for, we must enter into that state where we feel that He is "closer than breathing, nearer than hands and feet;" but it is only through faith that we may enter that sublime state.

While in faith we know that the Infinite is just as desirous to give as we are to receive; and this is absolutely necessary to know and feel, because if we doubt the desire of God to give, or believe that he must be persuaded and implored, our thought of God is wrong; we are out of harmony with God, and can not enter into His presence to receive what we have asked for.

It is for this reason that the prayer of the righteous availeth much; the righteous is in harmony with God, in perfect oneness with God, in right relations to God, and is therefore in the spirit, in the presence of God.

To be righteous means to be living the right life; and to live the right life is to live *with* God, to be so near to God that we feel His peaceful and loving presence at all times.

The righteous man has entered into such perfect oneness with the spirit that he can *feel* that he is living, moving and having his being in the very life of the Supreme. He is, therefore, in the secret places of the Most High, and is so near the throne that he may receive whatever he desires to ask for.

All things that are necessary to the perfect life of man have already been given to man; they are in store for man, in the spirit; and by entering the spirit he may receive them now.

"Whatsoever ye ask and pray for, believe that ye have received, and ye shall have it." No prayer is answered unless we believe that we have received; but faith believes because faith knows. Faith lives in the spirit and knows that anything that man may ask for is already in store for him. To pray is therefore not to stand apart from God and implore, but to enter into the spirit of God and receive from His loving kindness what He is more than willing to give.

Whatever we receive in the spirit that we also shall receive in the personal life, because whatever comes from the within draws unto itself, its own from the without.

We receive from the within only that which we realize we have received in the within; we must feel convinced that all our needs have already been supplied, and that the supply is waiting, in the great spiritual domain, for us to come and take possession; but this conviction comes only through faith, because faith is *in* the spirit and knows what the spirit has in store.

It is therefore simple to understand why the prayer of faith is always answered; and why those who live by faith have all their desires supplied.

Faith will invariably supply all your needs if you are doing something to justify those needs.

If you are engaged in a large undertaking, and are doing something that has value and worth, everything that you need to carry on that undertaking will be supplied, if you have faith.

Have no fear to begin any good work, no matter how great and extensive it may be; all the essentials will be supplied; your prayers will be answered if uttered in the spirit of faith.

In every phase of personal life the same is true; live a worthy life; live for something worth while, and everything you may need to make your own life as large, as ideal, as perfect and as beautiful as you may wish it to be, shall be supplied, and supplied without delay, if all your prayers are uttered in the spirit of faith.

It is prayer and faith united as one that produces the greatest power in the life of man; it is a power that is invincible, therefore, whatever we desire *in* faith, that we shall positively receive.

Desire wisdom, desire power, desire ability, desire gold and silver if you need them, desire everything necessary to a great and successful life, and have the faith that all your prayers will be answered.

Give your whole life to your desire, and express every desire *through* the very soul of faith; your desires shall be fulfilled, absolutely without fail. As your faith is, so shall it be unto you.

WHEN we enter the inner spirit of faith we discover that there is a higher power in man, and all about the being of man; in brief, we live and move in an infinite sea of higher power.

No matter how far we may go in the ascending scale of life, there is always a higher power that we may realize and appropriate for personal, tangible use.

To gain possession of this higher power, faith is the secret; because faith transcends all limitations; faith perpetually transcends; therefore, to live in faith is to pass eternally from the superior to that which is greater than the superior; from that which seems limitless to that which is infinitely larger and more sublime.

In the mind of the average person there is a belief that he is a limited personality, endowed with a certain amount of physical and mental energy; he believes that there is no way to increase that amount, therefore, stamps upon the subconscious the idea of the limitation he has fixed for himself.

The result is that he receives from the limitless source only as much power as his limited, circumscribed mentality can receive and appropriate; he is not aware of the fact that what he does receive comes from the limitless source; nor does he know that the supply received is limited simply because he *thinks* that his power is limited.

The law is that we receive from the source of limitless power only as much power as we think we possess; therefore, by expanding consciousness so as to realize a larger measure of power we begin to receive this larger measure.

The average person is also unaware of the fact that the supply of power will increase as he prepares to receive the increase, and that he may receive from the limitless source as much power as he can possibly hold in consciousness.

However, when the mind, through faith, rises above its previous circumscribed states, and enters more closely into touch with the Supreme, the truth concerning the entire subject of power is realized.

We then find that we are not endowed with a certain limited amount of life and power that remains fixed, and that perpetuates itself through physical processes during a temporal, personal existence; we find, to the contrary, that we receive daily, and hourly, from the boundless, as much power as we can consciously comprehend at the time; or as much as we have the capacity to receive and appropriate in our present state of consciousness of power.

As consciousness ascends into a higher and a more perfect realization of the eternal and the limitless, the mind is opened more and more to the power that exists in the boundless state; and as the nearness between the individual mind and the Supreme is perfected, the greater capacity to live, to think and to do is realized.

The nearer we feel that we are to the Infinite, the more life and power we receive from the limitless source; and it is through faith that this nearness is attained.

The same law holds in the worlds of freedom, purity, health, harmony, wisdom, joy and love. The nearer we *feel* we are to the Infinite, the more of these qualities we receive.

The nearer we feel we are to the higher realms the more fully we are conscious of what exists for us in those realms; and the more we are conscious of the more we receive, because whatever we become conscious of that we bring forth into possession and expression.

Every soul should learn to open the mind fully to this higher power, and should never undertake anything without securing the largest possible measure of those energies that come direct from the limitless source.

We shall find that our best and largest work is always done while we are conscious of the immensity of this power within us, and all about us.

All great minds have been inspired and pressed on to remarkable achievements through feeling the presence of this superior power; and it is this power that is responsible for the greatest deeds that the world has seen.

When you realize the presence of this power you feel that you are something more than human; you feel that you are not only a genius, but that you are a giant in mind and soul; you feel that there is a supreme something within you, and this something thrills your entire being with the conviction that nothing is impossible; you feel that you are able to be everything you ever imagined yourself to be, and infinitely more. You are in that world where the limitless actually does exist, and you feel as one that *is* limitless.

By entering into the life of this higher power, and by depending upon this power at all times, you will positively achieve greatness; and you will discover that this power is your own; your own unbounded power, awakened from the great within.

By depending upon higher power you

are depending upon yourself—your whole self; you are recognizing the great truth that what is in God is in you, and that all things that belong to the Supreme belong to Man—the image and likeness of the Supreme.

To depend upon higher power is not dependence, but the opening of the mind to the limitless life from within. It is therefore the direct path to the highest individual development.

Through the constant appropriation of higher power the small mind becomes great, the ordinary mind becomes a genius, and those who already have ability may double and treble the rare talents they now possess.

To constantly live in the consciousness of higher power will give this power to every thought that mind may create; a fact of extreme importance, because every Man, in the personal sense, is the product of his thought.

Through the power of thought anything in the personal life can be changed; but the power of the thought must be equal to every occasion.

It is through thought that man changes himself, changes his environment and creates his own destiny; therefore, if he is to do all that he desires to do, the power of his thought must be limitless.

To live and think in the consciousness of higher power will give unlimited power to thought, and enable the mind to exercise complete mastery over life; and it is through faith that the consciousness of higher power is gained; therefore, nothing is impossible to him who has faith.

When every thought is filled with higher power, nothing but good will come from thought, however powerful the thought may be, because all higher power is constructive, elevating and emancipating. This power *is* harmony, peace, health, purity and perfection, and gives richly of itself to everything with which it may come in contact.

Since man is constantly thinking, the good that will come when every thought has higher power, can never be measured.

The thought that has power is the thought that is created in faith; the thought that is formed while we *feel* the presence of higher power.

The strong thought is born of the spirit, and of the spirit only; and it is through faith that we enter the spirit.

It is such thought that heals, and when we learn to create all our thought in the realization of higher power, every person to whom we may give our healing thought will find emancipation.

It is the strong thought that heals, but

the strong thought is not that thought that is driven by will-force; thoughts that come from will-force are the weakest of all, and seldom accomplish anything.

The strong thought is the thought that is created in the *silent realization of unbounded power.*

Such thought has healing on its wings; such thought will fill the body with health, purity and power; such thought will produce complete emancipation wherever its power may be directed; such thought will smoothen the pathway of life, harmonize all the elements of existence, and build for man a vigorous body, a strong character, a powerful mind and an invincible soul.

Be still, and know that you are in the presence of a power that is supreme, a power that can do all things, and every thought you think will contain this power, and will do with this power whatever your heart may desire to have done.

To secure more power do not try to force the power you may already possess, but enter those higher spiritual realms, through faith, where power is limitless; and when you enter that state your thoughts not only become enormously strong, but thinking becomes so smooth and so gentle that you think the most wonderful thoughts and the most powerful thoughts, **even** without any effort whatever.

When we have great and difficult undertakings before us, we should remain calm, and permit supreme power to enter our thoughts; difficulties will instantaneously disappear, the work will almost do itself, and the goal in view will be reached with as perfect ease as the simplest task we ever performed.

The great achievement will be the result of higher power; not a power coming to us from some separate, outside source, but a higher power all our own—our own unbounded power, awakened from the limitless within.

Experience teaches that it is not strenuous nor laborious thinking that produces the greatest results in life, but those high, strong thoughts we create while we are in the secret places—in the peace that passeth understanding.

The hidden path to these secret places is faith; to enter faith is to enter the life of higher power, supreme power, limitless power; to enter faith is to enter the very soul of existence and gain possession of that something that produces all the worth, all the goodness and all the beauty of eternal life; to enter faith is to enter that rare and wonderful something that is prepared for them that love Him.

Eye hath not seen, nor ear heard; neither has it entered into the heart of man; but faith knows; faith has found the hidden way; and those who follow faith shall pass through the gates ajar and shall meet Him face to face.

Not in the distant future, in some other sphere of existence; but now, to-day; the kingdom of heaven is within you, and faith is the hidden secret to its splendor, its glory and its infinite joy.

To have faith in faith is to open the mind to an inner world of sublime existence—a life of indescribable beauty and unfathomable joy. It is this life of which we gain occasional glimpses while we are on the mountain top of spiritual thought; and it is in these states that we behold that something that tongue can never picture nor the mind of man understand.

At rare intervals we pass within the pearly gates; we touch the hem of His garment; we are transformed by the presence of His shining glory, and life is not the same any more. We have been in the cosmic state; we have seen real life; and we offer eternal thanksgiving because we are blessed with the privilege of existence; a privilege so great, that to live—simply to live—that is sufficient.

As we grow in faith we come nearer and nearer to this sublime state of existence, until we dwell on the borderland of its splendor nearly every hour. Later, we may pass the borderland whenever we so desire, and live almost constantly on that fair eternal shore.

Again, we must remember, that this life is not for some future state of existence; this life is for to-day; and faith is the perfect way; faith is the hidden secret to the marvelous splendor of the cosmic state.

To train ourselves to live in these beautiful serene realms, where simply to live is everlasting joy, we must learn to be still; never to force anything, but to so live that we constantly depend upon infinite power to come forth and do what the heart may desire to have done.

It is while living in this state that we feel the real presence of higher power—invincible power; and it is by giving full and free expression to this power that we transcend all limitations and demonstrate the great truth that all things are possible.

To enter this state faith is the secret—the hidden secret; but hidden no more from those who have faith in faith.

To enter faith, turn mind upon the inner side of life, and mentally dwell upon the inner reality that permeates all things. This reality may be termed a shining reality because it is the very essence of light, purity and perfection.

When you are in faith your mind actually

enters into this essence, and thereby awakens the unbounded life that absolute reality contains.

It is for this reason that faith can see you through anything; no matter what your obstacles or difficulties may be, simply have faith; faith will see you through. Live in the faith that everything is coming the way you desire, and as your faith is, so shall it be.

Do not permit fear or doubt to enter mind when things fail to look as bright as you may wish; judge not according to appearances; have faith; faith can change anything in your favor, and turn everything to good account for you.

When faith seems to fail, have more faith; and have more faith in faith; you will thereby produce a turn in the lane, because faith can produce anything; faith opens the mind to limitless power, therefore, we can never doubt the power of faith.

When in doubt, have faith, more faith; enter into the very soul of faith and the dawn you have been waiting for shall immediately appear.

Whatever the indications may be, they signify nothing in the presence of faith; faith can turn any failure into the greatest success; faith can lay its hands upon anything that is going backward, and cause it to move forward more rapidly than any undertaking has moved before.

Let not your heart be troubled in the presence of unfavorable indications; simply have faith; faith will see you through; faith never fails; faith can do anything, providing we continue ceaselessly in faith, and have abundance of faith in the limitless power of faith.

AITH is not for a part of life; faith is for the whole of life; therefore, the power of faith should be applied to every phase of practical every-day living; but to secure the best results from faith in daily, objective work we must not look upon external success as a material, inferior product.

All things are good when turned to good account; and all success will be turned to good account when we live, think and work in faith.

Faith does not stand apart from the physical world, waiting to minister to certain obscure spiritual wants only; faith is ready to turn its power into everything and has the power to produce success through everything; but faith will not cooperate with those things that are looked down upon and condemned by man.

The power of faith does not work apart from present physical means and methods; but uses these methods for the attainment of the highest results that are possible now.

You do not have to change your occupation to introduce faith into practical life; if your occupation is legitimate, remain where you are; use the methods you have used before, no matter how material they may seem to be; make no startling changes in the without; meet the world in the usual way, and deal with the world in a way that the world can understand, knowing that all things are good that are turned to good account; but make this change—give your occupation soul by working in faith.

By working in faith you bring forth a greater power from within, a power that will permeate every part of your occupation, a power that will expand, enlarge and develop your business, a power that will purify your business and elevate the entire undertaking to a higher plane.

Upon this higher plane your efforts will be promoted on a far more extensive scale, you will have greater success than ever before, the products of your work will be superior in worth, value and quality, and your usefulness to the race will become greater and greater in proportion.

The industrial world will not be purified by making changes in the without, but by awakening the higher powers from within; the man who enters the industrial world may not expect to reach his goal in view by hard work on the surface, but by permeating his work with limitless power from within.

This he may do by having faith in his work; by thinking of his work as good, not material, and by having such a perfect faith in faith that fear concerning results is entirely eliminated from his mind.

The greatest obstacle to real, true success in any sphere of human endeavor is fear—fear concerning results; faith removes this fear absolutely, therefore, *faith is indispensable in the industrial world.*

No man is equipped for any undertaking in life unless he has faith—the real, living faith; the faith that does things; the faith that can make all things possible.

IN the attitude of faith the mind sees the ideal, the real, the perfect, and patterns all thinking according to the vision of that greater life; and since man is as he thinks, by thinking greater thoughts he becomes a greater man.

In the attitude of fear the imagination pictures all kinds of false, imperfect, inferior and even monstrous forms of thought; all of these work themselves out in mind, character and personal life, thereby burdening the system with all kinds of detrimental conditions. Such conditions interfere so seriously with everything that man may try to do, that the failure he feared must inevitably follow.

To follow faith is to move forward steadily and surely, even under the most adverse and trying conditions; to follow fear is to go down to failure and defeat even under the most favorable conditions in existence.

To banish fear, have faith; the only infallible remedy for fear is faith; faith in all things, and at all times.

Faith sees the substance and gains the substance; fear sees the shadow and is soon left with nothing but the shadow.

The man who fears looks upon the lesser, thereby becoming lesser for every passing day; the man who has faith keeps the eye single upon the larger, thereby entering the path of perpetual increase.

Fear, by looking down, compels the mind to create the lower; faith, by looking up, causes the mind to create the superior.

Fear expects the human side to prevail, and believes the worst is coming, thereby causing the weak human side to prevail, and bringing the worst to pass. Faith continues to believe that the divine side will prevail, thereby causing the divine side to gain supremacy.

When mind is in the attitude of faith there is no fear of adversity; there is not even any thought of adversity, because while in faith the mind is above all adverseness; it is in peace, harmony and rightness; it is in the life of that power that can, and does cause everything to move smoothly, and all things to work together for good.

While in faith the mind has no fear of failure; faith never thinks of failure; faith sees the possibilities of success; faith knows that success in every instance is possible because it knows that all things are possible; faith does not ask if success will come, but opens the mind to the great power within that positively will produce success.

When in the attitude of faith the mind has no fear whatever, because fear, in any form, is absolutely out of the question when you realize that you live and move and have your being in the spirit of the Infinite; and to enter faith is to enter completely into this high and wonderful realization.

When the mind is in fear, attention is centered upon evil; when the mind is in faith, attention is centered upon the good; therefore, fear creates evil in mind and character, while faith creates only the good. We always think about that upon which our attention is centered; and what we think about that we create in our own mentalities.

This being true, we can readily understand why the things we fear come upon us, and why we always receive the things we desire in faith.

To desire, with the whole heart and soul, what we need or wish for, and to place unbounded faith in that desire, will in every instance produce results.

This principle can be applied to everything on all planes of life; there is therefore, no reason why any one should ever want for anything.

Faith is the hidden secret to all supply, and he who enters faith, by having faith in faith, will find the world of limitless supply.

To the mind of mere reason this may not seem true, but it is true; faith knows it to be true, and the light of faith is higher than the light of reason. It is, therefore, well in the beginning, not to reason too much about the why's and the wherefore's of faith.

To reason about that which the outer mind can not understand will confuse consciousness and prevent that serene state of perfect assurance which is necessary to faith.

Know that faith can do everything; and know that faith will reveal to you exactly how it is done; then have more faith; ere long, faith will become so strong that even reason will be convinced, and will co-operate with faith in demonstrating to the outer mind that the claims of faith are true—absolutely true.

What you do not understand leave to faith; faith is the hidden secret to all understanding, and by having faith in faith, the secret of everything will be revealed to you.

Since faith is the hidden secret, to enter into faith is to enter into this same secret; henceforth, nothing will be hidden from you.

To him who lives in faith there are no

problems; life is clear, the purpose of life is clear, the law of living the life is clear, the path to endless ascension in life is clear—everything is clear; and it is also clear that all things will be according to the measure of faith.

FAITH knows; faith is not blind; faith is in the real light and sees everything; faith is never misled, because it is a superior vision, a keener insight and a higher understanding. It is therefore safe to follow faith, and whenever we follow faith wherever faith may go, whatever comes will be good—very good.

All things will work together for good when we live in faith, and constantly follow the light of faith.

Whatever you undertake to do, expect to be guided by faith, have faith in the superior wisdom of faith, and depend upon faith to give you the insight that knows when to act, and the power required to secure the very best and the very greatest results. You positively can not fail, because as your faith is, so shall it be.

When you have found your work, have faith, and press on. Do not stop to wonder if you are to succeed; have the faith that you will succeed, and nothing in the world can prevent you from reaching the very highest goal you may have in view.

Do not wonder what is going to happen, but proceed to create those events and circumstances that will be favorable to the purpose you have in mind. This anyone can do who works with the Infinite, and works *in* faith.

Do not wait for things to come your way; take hold of things and turn them the way they ought to be; faith will give you the power.

When things go wrong, have faith; depend upon faith to set them right, and the limitless power that is back of faith will appear to fulfill your desire.

When in the midst of changes expect every change to be an open door to better things than you ever knew before; live in that faith; permeate your whole heart, your whole life and your whole soul with that faith, and as your faith is, so shall it be.

When you have obligations to meet, bills to pay, and have not the essentials required, have faith; never worry nor feel anxious for a moment; know that faith can open to you the realms of limitless supply, and know that faith will do this if you have faith in faith.

Whatever you need place the matter in the hands of faith; faith will find a way; faith will reveal to you the necessary opportunities through which you may accomplish what you desire and meet your obligations. Do not ask how, simply depend upon faith; you will soon know how; have faith in faith and the hidden secrets of faith will be fully revealed to you.

Never be disturbed if results should fail to appear at once; know that faith will open the way before it is too late; and the same shall positively be done.

Again, we must remember not to depend simply upon a mere belief in faith, but to mentally dwell in the very soul of faith.

When you have faith in things, take heart and mind and soul into the real spirit of things and you enter the spirit of faith; you enter real faith—the hidden secret, and the great secret is hidden to you no more.

Faith never fails when you enter into the soul of faith while having faith; this is one of the greatest of all truths; and the man who accepts this truth will have unlimited power placed at his command.

To enter faith is to enter the life of the limitless power that is within us and all about us; to have faith—real faith, is to open the mind to the influx of that power from within that can do all things; therefore, to have faith—the deep, strong, soul-faith, is to reduce failures to nothing.

This is another great truth that should be proclaimed from every housetop, and re-echoed throughout the world.

Have faith, and whatever you may

undertake to do, that you shall surely accomplish. Limitless power can not fail, and faith opens the mind to that power.

This proves conclusively that faith is the hidden secret—the very secret of all secrets.

Faith has the secret, therefore it pays no attention to appearances nor external indications; faith works upon the principle that whatever we have the desire to accomplish, that we have the power to accomplish; faith works upon this principle because it knows that there is unbounded power in man; and faith also knows that man can gain conscious possession of this power by having faith in faith.

One of the greatest essentials to the attainment of the more beautiful life is to realize the reality of the real; and to produce this realization is one of the principal functions of faith.

Faith is interior understanding; faith can look beyond the world of sense and see things as they are; faith can see what is in the real, what can be done through the realization of the real, what ought to be done to express the real, and how this may be done now; or what should be done now to work up to the high ideals we may have in view.

If you wish to realize your ideals follow faith; faith will guide you perfectly, and provide everything you may require to reach your lofty goal.

Faith always brings us into harmony with the inner, finer essence of things; hence its enormous power.

Faith opens the door to the great unknown, and proves that the great unknown is simply an extension—an endless extension, of that which is known.

Faith is the evidence of things not seen, because faith does see what has not been seen; faith knows that the unseen is real and substantial; faith proves that the unseen can be seen by those who will awaken the superior mind within; therefore, by entering into faith we enter into the realization of the real and see all things as they are in the perfect state.

Faith proves that the great unknown is unknown only to those who have not begun to live the larger life; but to follow faith is to enter the new life, because faith goes on and reveals the wonders and the powers of the larger spheres of existence; not simply those spheres that may exist beyond the scope of sense, but also those spheres that exist all about us, here and now, within the very world of sense.

In every vocation, in every study and in every field of thought, there are new worlds of unbounded possibilities, which when discovered and developed will add immeasurably to the real worth of life.

Never yearn for new worlds to conquer, nor complain because there are no opportunities at hand for you; there are a million worlds—rich, marvelous worlds at your very door; turn your attention to these and you shall have opportunities without number, not simply for the present, but for ages yet to be.

The hidden secret to these new worlds is faith; enter faith and a new universe shall be given to you; a universe that is more real and substantial than anything you have known before; a universe that is marvelous in beauty, and filled with possibilities more numerous than the sands of the shore.

In faith consciousness is constantly on the verge of the great unknown, receiving glimpses of the great beyond; when faith disappears our visions of greater things are gone; but when faith returns again we see the same marvels, and know that we shall tangibly possess them in the coming days.

To try to become conscious of something that is beyond the present capacity of consciousness, produces a shock to the mind; a fact that every one knows who has tried to comprehend the universe with the limitations of the personal mind; but when the mind works and thinks in faith, consciousness expands constantly, naturally and of its own accord, thus producing perpetual and normal growth of mind.

To understand the universe, to understand God, to understand life—these things are impossible without faith; to try to do so simply shocks the mind; but in faith these things are readily understood without the slightest mental effort. High truths come as clear, vivid revelations to the mind that thinks in faith.

Faith does not simply believe; faith knows; real faith *is* a superior understanding, and deals with tangible facts on all planes.

It is not the function of faith to blindly accept, but to give man the wisdom, and the power to do greater things. Real faith goes to work, but asks no questions about results. Faith knows that all is possible now, and acts accordingly. Faith enters the larger life and takes up the greater undertakings as if there were no obstacles, and discovers that obstacles can not exist anywhere.

The only semblance of obstacles that can be found are the limitations that we believe to exist within our own conscious actions. Consciousness goes out so far, reaches so far, and where it ends to-day we imagine our obstacle to be. We fear to go on farther because beyond the reach of present consciousness there seems to be nothing. There seems to be nothing because we have not gone on any farther to see; but when we follow faith and press on, we find the seeming void to be solid rock.

Faith knows that the obstacle we think we see is an illusion; it does not exist in reality; it is only a belief produced by our inability to reach any further than we do; but faith dispels this belief; faith leads consciousness on in every direction, and proves to mind that we may go as far as we like anywhere, we shall find substantial footing everywhere, without a single obstacle in the way.

Faith knows that there is something everywhere; and to him who has faith this something is revealed.

For this reason faith is the substance of things hoped for; faith enters into the very life and substance of that which is desired, thereby finding the substance and gaining possession of the coveted treasure.

Faith is the hidden secret, therefore is *in* the substance of all things; to have faith in things is to enter into the substance of things, into the secret life of things; faith is the soul, the inner substance of all mental actions, of all desires and hopes; therefore faith is the substance of things hoped for, and brings that substance into tangible possession.

No thought should end in hope; the thought that ends in hope produces failure; the thought that passes from hope to faith will succeed under any and every circumstance. The reason why is most evident.

Hope stands on the outside, faith walks in; hope waits to be guided, faith trusts in its own light and proceeds; hope expects to receive external help, faith awakens its own limitless powers and produces results without help; hope is ever waiting for things to come right, faith goes to work and turns all things into the right; hope hopes for the best, faith lives and works in the faith that the best must come, thereby creating the best and the best only.

Faith can do all things because it uses all things and works in harmony with all things. Faith enters into the very life of life, and is therefore *in* the soul of life; to be in the soul of life is to feel, realize and receive the life that contains all power, all wisdom and all love.

Through faith man can do all things, because faith awakens that something in man that can do all things.

If ye have faith as a grain of mustard seed, ye shall say unto this mountain, Remove hence to yonder place; and it shall remove; and nothing shall be impossible unto you.

This remarkable statement, coming from the greatest mind that has appeared upon earth, offers more evidence—absolutely conclusive evidence, to substantiate the assertion that faith is the hidden secret.

No attainment is therefore greater than the attainment of faith; neither can any other attainment reach its highest state of efficiency, perfection and power, unless it is based upon faith, animated by faith and developed through faith. The highest and best can never be reached without faith, because faith alone is the hidden secret to all that is high, worthy and superior in man.

Faith does not come to take the place of other attainments; faith comes to give real soul and higher power to every attainment; and to awaken in man possibilities he has never known before.

Faith does not come to supersede skill, intellect and ability, nor to reduce work to a minimum; faith comes to unite all work, all skill and all ability with the limitless powers of the great within; therefore, the man who unites these three—work, ability and faith—shall accomplish everything he may undertake to do. When these three are made *One,* failure is annihilated completely, and the greatest success is positively in store.

Work with the most perfect skill that you can possibly develop, but fill your work with the limitless power of unbounded faith; become as learned, as intellectual and as highly cultured in mind as possible, but illumine that prodigious intellect with the radiant spirit of faith; make the fullest use of all physical functions and all mental talents, but animate every action of mind and body with the invincible power of faith.

Give faith to everything, have faith in everything, unite faith with everything, and everything shall be filled with that power that makes all things possible.

If you wish to reach the highest places that life has in store for man have faith, and your wish shall positively come true. It is faith that awakens the higher and greater within you, thereby elevating all your faculties to the highest state of efficiency; it is faith that opens the mind to that superior power that alone can create the prodigy and the genius; it is faith that gives such a rare quality to everything you do that both you and your work are stamped universally with the mark of high worth.

It is faith that fills the soul with that strange determination that carries you on and on through all sorts of conditions, and finally brings you to the very mountaintop of attainment and achievement.

It is faith alone that produces real greatness; that greatness that can never die, but forever remains as an inspiration to all the world.

What the personal man is to-day matters nothing; where the personal man may live to-day matters nothing; faith can change everything.

Have faith, and sorrow, sickness, trouble and misfortune shall vanish completely; all mountains shall be removed, and nothing shall be impossible unto you.

Have faith, and all your desires shall positively be fulfilled; faith and desire united as *One* can bring anything, produce anything, create anything, and cause anything to transpire in the life of man.

Faith gives invincible power to everything; faith is the hidden secret to all power; therefore, to enter faith is to enter the secret of faith, and the secret is hidden from you no more; the great within is opened before you, and unlimited power is at your command.

"Come where glory waits thee," this is the call of faith; not in some other sphere of existence, but here and now. Follow faith, and you shall enter greatness and power, wealth and glory, wisdom and genius, worth and superiority, peace and joy.

Enter faith—the very soul of faith, and you enter into the very presence of the Infinite, thereby placing yourself *in* the very life, the very power, the very wisdom and the very love of God. God will therefore be with you in everything you may undertake to do; and when God is with you, nothing is impossible. You *feel* His presence, and you are filled with His life at all times; this life is supreme, limitless, invincible; therefore, everything must pass before it that your prayer may be answered and His will be done.

To enter into the very soul of faith is to speak to the Infinite in the beautiful language of faith; and this is the prayer of faith; Infinite Father, I thank Thee that Thou hearest my prayer; I thank Thee that Thou hearest me always. I thank Thee that Thou hast already given me all that my heart can wish for, all that my life may need, for the time that is and the eternity that is to be; and now, with supreme joy and unspeakable thanksgiving, I come to Thee to receive Thy gifts, and receive from Thy loving hands the divine blessings that Thou hast, from all eternity, treasured for me.

This is the prayer of faith; this is the prayer that is always answered; this is the prayer without ceasing; the prayer that becomes a consecrated life—the life that is lived *with* God.

Faith is in the spirit; faith knows that God has given us everything now, and that it is His will that all our prayers should be answered now. Everything that we may need to live the full life, the perfect life, the beautiful life—the life that is fairer than ten thousand to the soul—everything that is necessary to this life, is ready for us in His kingdom now; but we must enter into His presence to receive our own, and faith is the gates ajar.

Faith is the hidden secret to every desire and need of man; therefore, all things are possible to him who has faith; and all things desired shall come to him who lives, thinks and acts *in* the very soul of that faith that *is* faith.

CPSIA information can be obtained
at www.ICGtesting.com
Printed in the USA
BVHW011708180621
609726BV00022B/1411